# TOPIC BOX

# Castles

**Pam Robson**

**Wayland**

## Titles in this Series
Castles
Dinosaurs
Fairs and Circuses
Houses and Homes
Minibeasts
My Body
The Seasons
Transport

This book was prepared for Wayland (Publishers) Ltd
by Globe Education, Nantwich, Cheshire

Design Concept by Pinpoint
Book Design by Steven Wheele Design
Artwork by Deborah Kindred

First published in 1995 by
Wayland (Publishers) Ltd
61 Western Road, Hove
East Sussex BN3 1JD

Printed and bound in Italy by
L.E.G.O. S.p.A., Vincenza

**British Library Cataloguing in Publication Data**

Robson, Pam
Castles. – (Topic Box Series)
I. Title II. Series
728.8109

ISBN 0 7502 1296 9

**Picture acknowledgements**
Bridgeman Art Library 13 (Bibliotheque Nationale), 16 (Lambeth Palace Library), 25 (Bibliotheque Nationale)
Life File 5 (Emma Lee), 8 (F. Ralston), 28 (Cliff Threadgold)
Mary Evans 15
Michael Holford 7
National Trust 29 (Bill Batten)
Peter Newarks' Historical Pictures 14, 26, 27
Zefa 10, 19t, 19b, 20 (and front cover), 21t, 21b (and title page), 24, 25b

# Contents

# What is a Castle?

Most castles were built in the Middle Ages. Powerful lords lived with their knights inside castles with high walls to keep them safe from their enemies. Many castles had a drawbridge and a moat.

Slowly, over the years life became more peaceful and less dangerous. Armed guards were no longer needed.

Some castles are still lived in, others are museums and some are ruins.

(Below) Castles are large, strong buildings with high walls. These are some of the features often found in castle buildings.

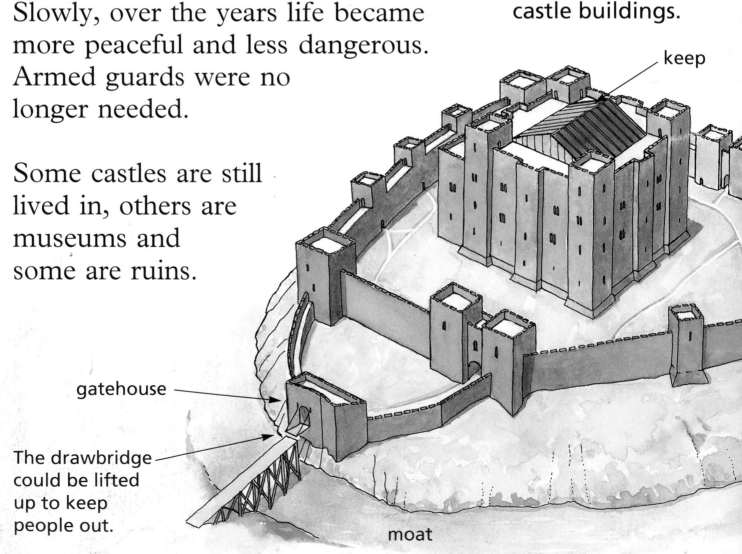

keep

gatehouse

The drawbridge could be lifted up to keep people out.

moat

(Above) Heidelberg Castle in Germany is no longer lived in but people often go to look around the old walls.

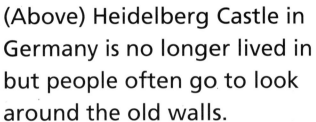

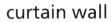
— curtain wall

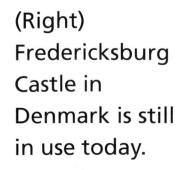

(Right) Fredericksburg Castle in Denmark is still in use today.

(Above) The portcullis could be lowered to protect the main entrance.

# Powerful Lords

When William of Normandy invaded England in 1066, he brought with him many powerful lords and their knights.

To keep control of those people who did not want a Norman king, he gave each of his powerful lords a castle.

The first of these castles were wooden forts, but wooden forts could be set on fire by enemies. Soon William began to build stronger castles with stone walls.

(Below) The simplest castles had a courtyard, known as a bailey, where people lived and worked, and a mound, known as a motte, where they could go for safety if attacked.

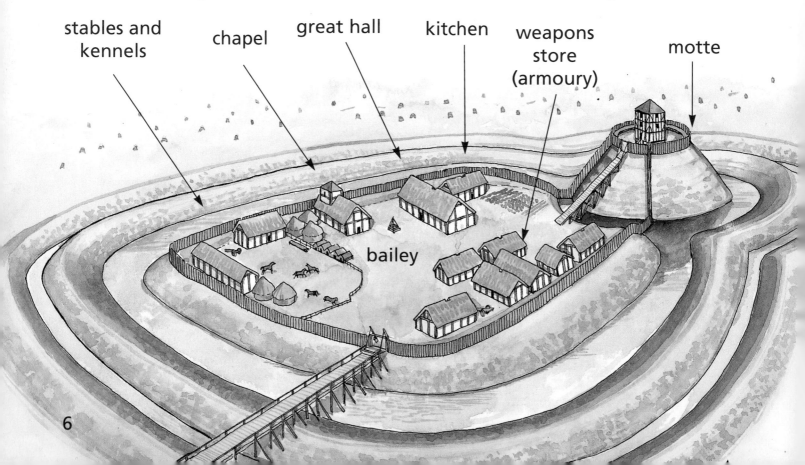

stables and kennels

chapel

great hall

kitchen

weapons store (armoury)

motte

bailey

(Right) Everyone in the castle ate together in the great hall.

(Below) The palisade was a high fence made of wooden posts with sharp ends.

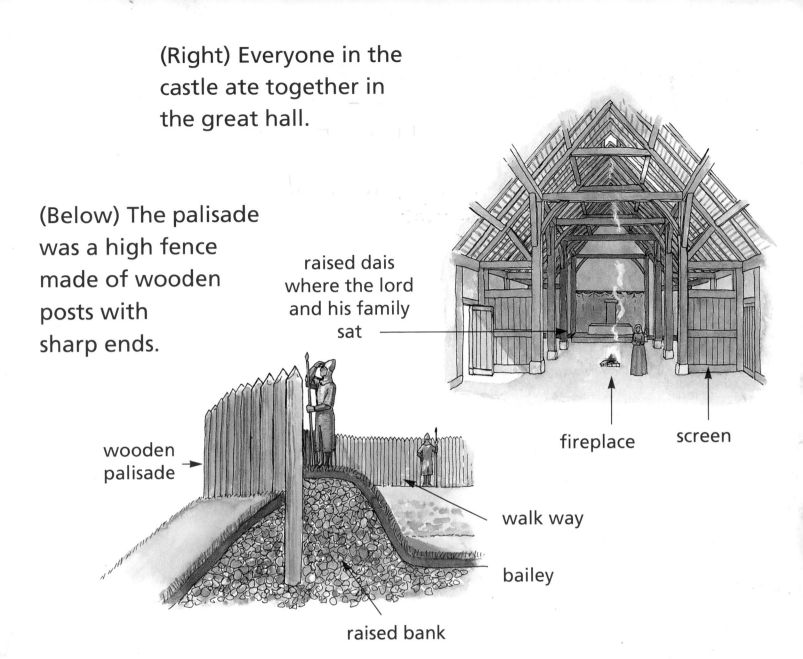

raised dais where the lord and his family sat

fireplace

screen

wooden palisade

walk way

bailey

raised bank

(Left) The Bayeux Tapestry tells the story of the Norman invasion of England. It shows Norman soldiers building a castle at Hastings.

# Choosing a Site

The site for a castle was chosen with great care. It had to be easy to defend and there had to be a good supply of drinking water for the people who would be living there.

Castles were often built on cliffs alongside rivers. From the top of a cliff, the guards could see enemies advancing. The river kept enemies out, provided drinking water and was an easy way of getting supplies and visitors to the castle by boat.

stone masons

Neuschwanstein Castle in Germany is built on high ground above a river.

hoist

ramp

**Building a castle needed many workmen.**

lord

site manager

mixing mortar

adze

hammer

chisel

auger

dividers

saw

Some of the tools used to build a castle.

# Castles in Stone

Many of the first stone castles had a strong square building called a keep.

The keep contained store-rooms, living quarters for the knights, the great hall, a chapel and rooms for the lord and his family. The only entrance was on the first floor. The windows were small with no glass. It was very gloomy and draughty inside.

Outside, a strong outer wall protected the bailey.

Work started on the square keep of Dover Castle in 1181.

The keep was like a fort. If the castle was attacked, people would shut themselves inside.

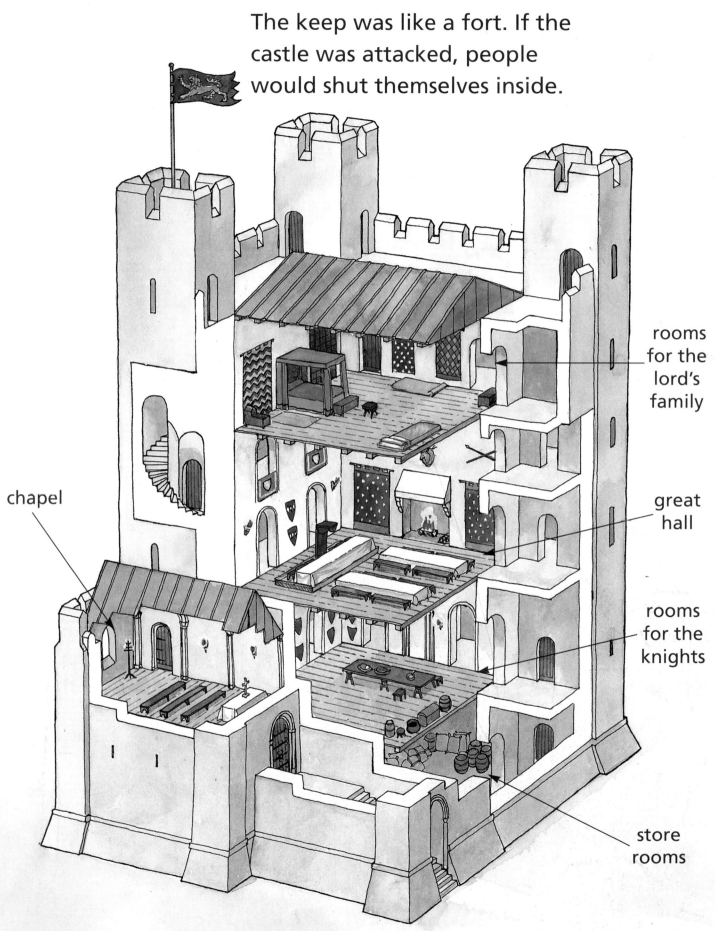

rooms for the lord's family

chapel

great hall

rooms for the knights

store rooms

# Castle Battles

Enemies would surround a castle in the hope that the people inside would surrender before they starved. This was called a siege.

Sometimes they used huge catapults to hurl rocks at the walls, or tree trunks to batter the doors.

The troops inside the castle would pour hot liquids over the walls on to their enemies, pelt them with stones and fire arrows at them.

gun port

belfry helped attackers to climb walls

castle wall

defenders' tunnel

attackers' tunnel

Sometimes attackers and defenders dug tunnels.

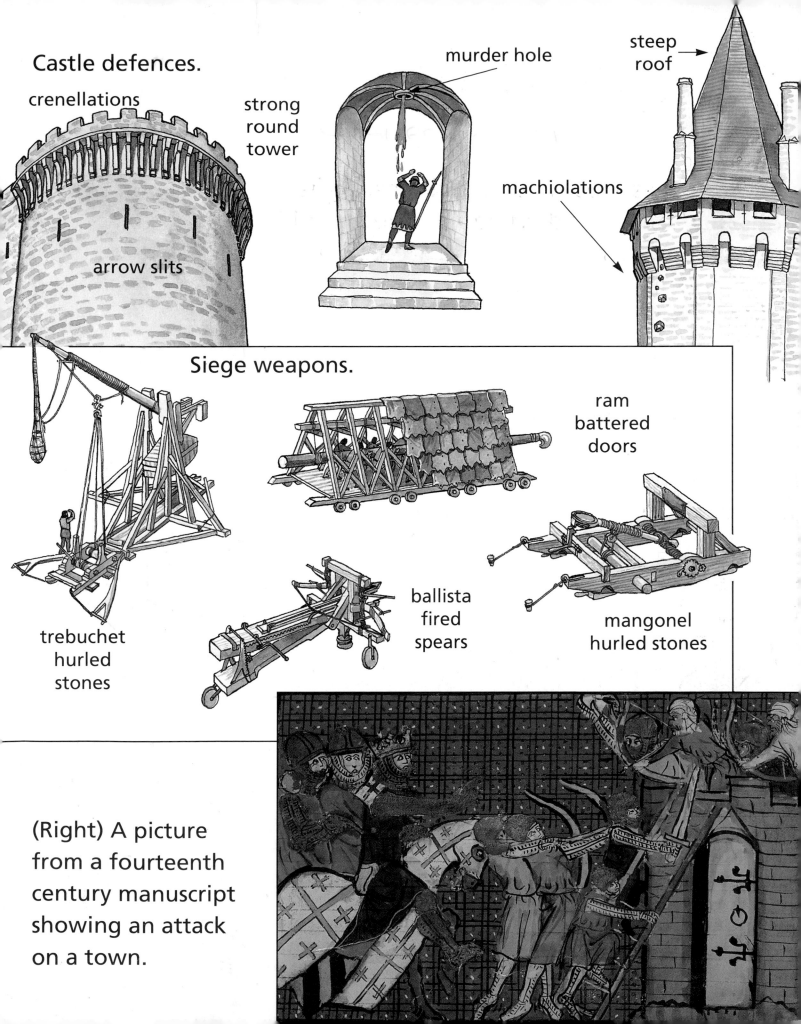

Castle defences.

crenellations

strong round tower

murder hole

steep roof

machiolations

arrow slits

Siege weapons.

ram battered doors

trebuchet hurled stones

ballista fired spears

mangonel hurled stones

(Right) A picture from a fourteenth century manuscript showing an attack on a town.

# Dark Dungeons

Castles made good prisons because they were strong and easy to defend. Prisoners were sometimes put in the storerooms below the keep as this was the strongest part of the castle.

The old Norman word for keep was donjon and because of this the prison later became known as the dungeon.

It was quite usual for prisoners to be tortured. Sometimes they were even murdered by their gaolers.

(Above and left) Prisoners might be tortured to make them admit to crimes.

(Right) Important people captured during battle were put in prison until ransom money was paid. This picture shows a French prince imprisoned in the Tower of London.

(Left) Sometimes prisoners were chained to the walls.

locking iron ring

Some castles had small prison cells with bars on doors and windows.

# Coats of Arms

In the Middle Ages, knights wore armour in battle. This made identification difficult, so each knight had a special design on his shield.

This design became known as a coat of arms. It was passed from father to son. Each important family had a coat of arms which they used to identify their property.

The study of arms is now known as heraldry.

Examples of coats of arms.

In this scene showing the Battle of Poitiers, the arms of the English Black Prince can be seen on the banner and the caparison (decorated covering) on his horse.

Armorial bearings.

Examples of shields.

A jousting competition.

Spectators recognized the knights by their coats of arms.

# Crusader Castles

The Crusades were holy wars that took place in the Middle Ages. Christian knights travelled from Europe to reclaim the Holy Land from Muslim invaders. They especially wanted to free the city of Jerusalem.

The knights were a long way from home so to protect themselves they built castles in strong positions. They used ideas they had seen in Muslim castles and later brought those ideas back to Europe.

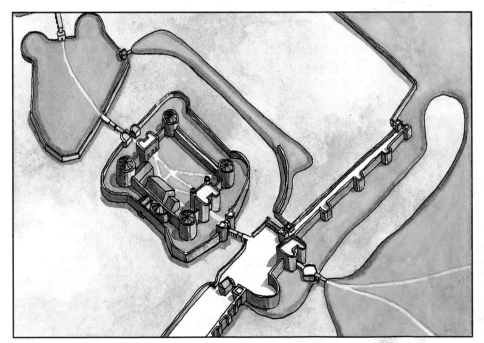

(Right) The Crusaders travelled thousands of miles to the Holy Land.

(Left) New castles had amazing defences.

The Crusaders built castles for themselves like this one at Bodrum in Turkey.

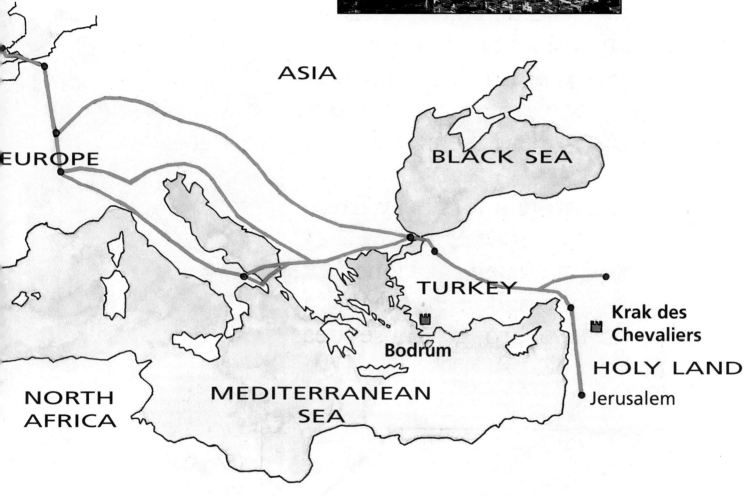

ASIA

BLACK SEA

EUROPE

TURKEY

Bodrum

Krak des Chevaliers

HOLY LAND

Jerusalem

NORTH AFRICA

MEDITERRANEAN SEA

The Muslim fortress at Krak des Chevaliers was occupied by the Crusaders. When they returned home they copied Muslim building methods.

# Castles in Spain

Muslim warriors invaded Spain in 711. They lived there for hundreds of years and built many castles that were stronger and more beautiful than any other European castles.

The Muslims built garrison forts known as alcazabas. They had high walls with many towers and ornate patterns in the stone.

Christian knights finally managed to recapture the whole of Spain in 1492.

The Alcázar at Segovia was built in the eleventh century. Its shape is very like a huge ship.

(Below) The map shows where in Spain you will find the castles pictured on these two pages.

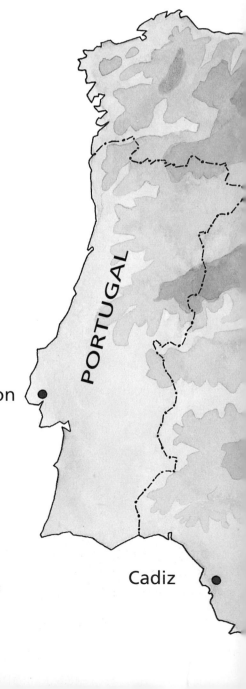

PORTUGAL

Lisbon

Cadiz

(Left) Coca Castle near to Segovia was built in the fifteenth century from brick. There are decorated crenellations on the top of the towers and walls.

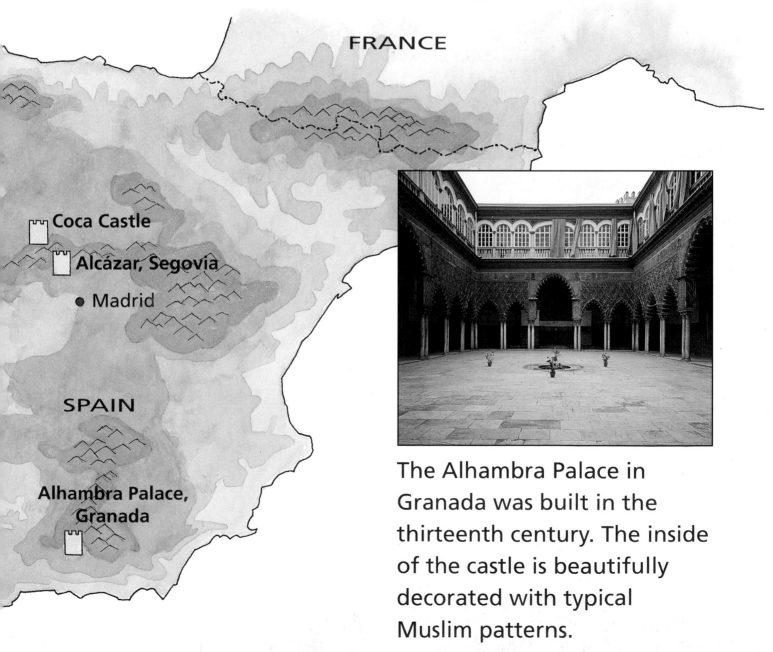

FRANCE

Coca Castle

Alcázar, Segovia

● Madrid

SPAIN

Alhambra Palace, Granada

The Alhambra Palace in Granada was built in the thirteenth century. The inside of the castle is beautifully decorated with typical Muslim patterns.

# Castle Life

By the fourteenth century, castle life had become more comfortable. The walls had plaster, windows had glass and the lord no longer lived in the keep.

The castle had become almost like a village. There were blacksmiths and carpenters, cooks and washerwomen grooms for the horses, priests and scribes.

Different households lived and worked in different parts of the building.

hall

armoury

ditch

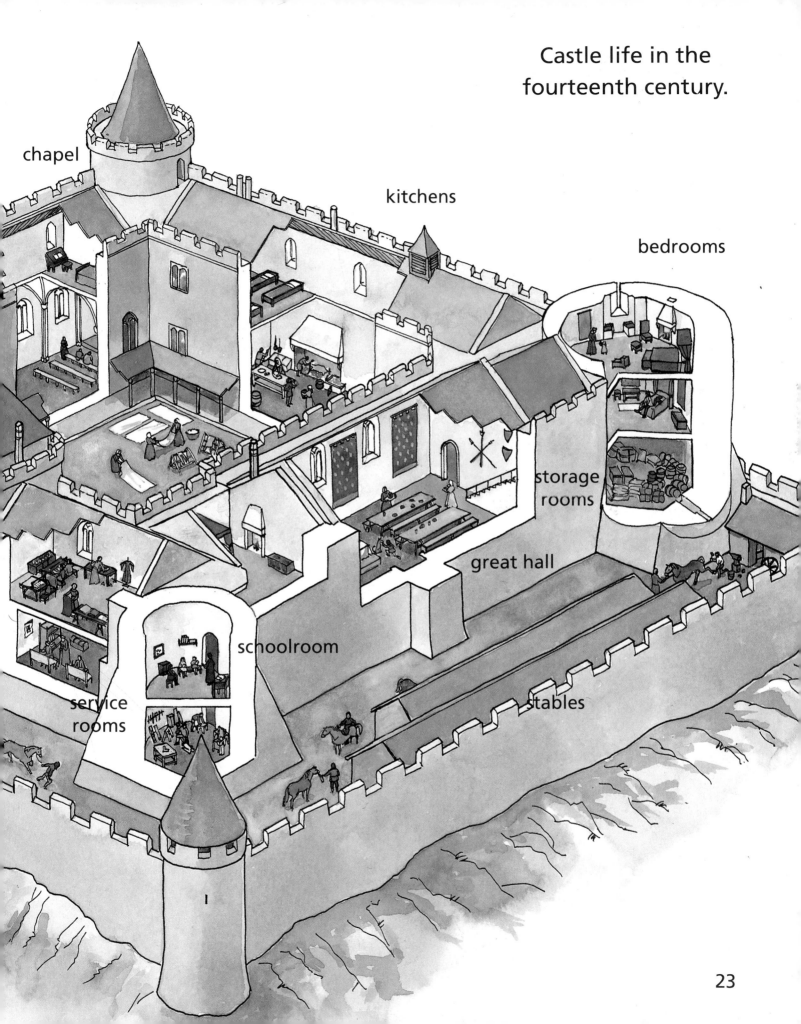

chapel

kitchens

bedrooms

storage rooms

great hall

schoolroom

service rooms

stables

Castle life in the fourteenth century.

# Time for Change

Castles were strong but could be damaged by cannon fire and often they were not rebuilt. Ways of fighting battles changed. They took place in open countryside and not around castle walls.

By the sixteenth century, castles were no longer important as homes because life had become much safer. Lords no longer needed to protect their families inside strong walls. They wanted warm, comfortable houses with gardens and parkland.

(Below) The castle at Chenonceaux in France became a comfortable house when the lord no longer needed to protect his family.

(Left) Corfe Castle in Britain was destroyed by cannon fire in the seventeenth century and never rebuilt.

(Right) This picture from a fifteenth century manuscript shows the Muslims using cannon fire to break the walls of the city of Rhodes.

(Right) Rheinsberg Castle at Brandenburg was built as a home, not to defend the lord and his family from his enemies.

# New World Castles

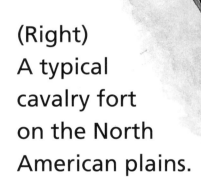

In the nineteenth century, log forts were built on the North American plains.

They were to protect new settlers from the Plains Indians who were angry at the invasion of their lands. Fort Laramie was one of the first and most important of these forts.

The Plains Wars lasted for over 40 years. Eventually, the Indians lost their land and their rights and the forts were no longer needed.

(Right)
A typical cavalry fort on the North American plains.

(Right and far right) Fort Laramie was first built by fur trappers and the Indians went there with furs to trade. Later, when the fur animals became scarce, the cavalry moved in to protect the settlers and drive out the Indians.

# Castles Today

Many castles are still standing today. You can visit castles that are now museums to find out what they are like inside.

Sometimes towers and walls have been added to a castle over the years changing its appearance.

Castle museums will also contain artefacts and exhibits explaining the routine of everyday castle life.

Tile from Samur Castle in France.

Typical French jug

(Left) The kitchen at Soligen Castle in Germany.

(Left) The outer hall at Dunster Castle in Britain.

(Above) Wheels used to lift water from the well at Samur Castle in France.

(Below) Oak chests were used as seats.

(Below) English pot used for medicine or jam.

# Word List

**Adze**   A hand tool used by carpenters to smooth wood.

**Auger**   A hand tool used by carpenters for boring holes in wood.

**Ballista**   A siege weapon that worked like a huge crossbow.

**Belfry**   A wooden tower on wheels that protected soldiers attacking castle walls.

**Caparison**   A decorated covering for a horse.

**Cavalry**   An army of soldiers mounted on horses.

**Coat of arms**   The designs and badges used to identify a family or group. Also known as the armorial bearings.

**Crenellations**   Gaps along the top of a castle wall that allowed soldiers standing on the walkway inside the wall to shoot at cnemies.

**Dais**   A raised platform.

**Donjon**   The fortified central keep of a medieval castle.

**Heraldry**   The science and art of a herald in creating coats of arms and settling the right to bear arms.

**Hoist**   A device for lifting materials and heavy weights.

**Holy Land**   An area of land, also known as Palestine, that is referred to in the Bible and is now part of Israel.

**Machiolations**   Holes in the floor of a gallery built on the outside of a castle wall. Soldiers could drop missiles through these holes on to their enemies.

**Mangonel**   A siege weapon used for hurling stones.

**Moat**   A water-filled ditch around a castle.

**Murder-hole**   An opening in the roof of an entrance passage to a castle that allowed soldiers to drop missiles on an enemy below.

**Muslim**   A follower of Islam.

**Palisade**   A strong wooden fence made of stakes driven into the ground

**Portcullis**   An iron or wooden grating that fitted into grooves each side of a castle gateway and could be lowered for protection.

**Ramp**   A sloping floor joining two places at different levels.

**Siege**   An act of war in which a fortified settlement is surrounded and regularly attacked to force surrender.

**Trebuchet**   A powerful long-range siege weapon with a sling that hurled stones.

# Finding Out More

## Places to Visit

British Museum,
Great Russell Street,
London WC1

Battle Abbey,
Hastings,
East Sussex

The many interesting castles built in the British Isles since the eleventh century are all worth visiting. Contact tourist information offices in the area of interest for further details.

## Books to Read

*A Medieval Castle*, Fiona Macdonald, (Macdonald Young Books, 1990)

*Castle*, Eyewitness Guide, (Dorling Kindersley, 1994)

*Castles*, Francesca Baines, (Watts, 1995)

*Castles*, R. Matthews, (Wayland, 1988)

*Castles and Mansions*, A. James, (Wayland, 1988)

*Seige,* Stewart Ross, (Wayland, 1995)

*The Builder Through History*, R. Wood, (Wayland, 1994)

*The Castle Story*, Sheila Sancha, (Collins, 1993)

*The Normans*, H. M. Martell, (Heinemann, 1992)

Guidebooks are usually on sale at castles open to the public.

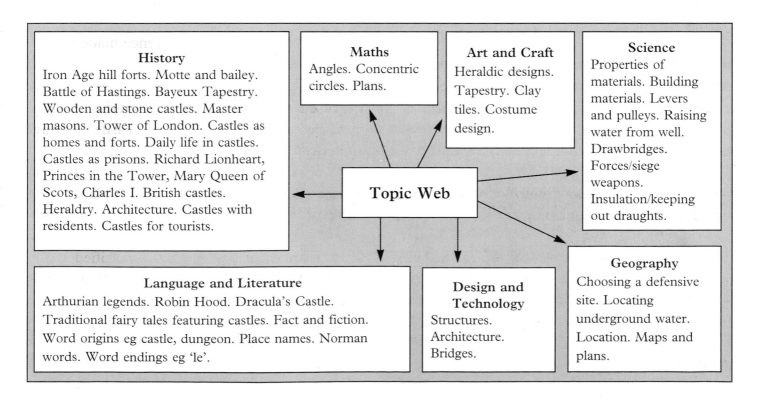

**History**
Iron Age hill forts. Motte and bailey. Battle of Hastings. Bayeux Tapestry. Wooden and stone castles. Master masons. Tower of London. Castles as homes and forts. Daily life in castles. Castles as prisons. Richard Lionheart, Princes in the Tower, Mary Queen of Scots, Charles I. British castles. Heraldry. Architecture. Castles with residents. Castles for tourists.

**Maths**
Angles. Concentric circles. Plans.

**Art and Craft**
Heraldic designs. Tapestry. Clay tiles. Costume design.

**Science**
Properties of materials. Building materials. Levers and pulleys. Raising water from well. Drawbridges. Forces/siege weapons. Insulation/keeping out draughts.

**Topic Web**

**Language and Literature**
Arthurian legends. Robin Hood. Dracula's Castle. Traditional fairy tales featuring castles. Fact and fiction. Word origins eg castle, dungeon. Place names. Norman words. Word endings eg 'le'.

**Design and Technology**
Structures. Architecture. Bridges.

**Geography**
Choosing a defensive site. Locating underground water. Location. Maps and plans.

# Index